INTERCITY 225
Class 91 Locomotives and Mark 4 Coaches

Rich Mackin

AMBERLEY

First published 2018

Amberley Publishing
The Hill, Stroud
Gloucestershire, GL5 4EP

www.amberley-books.com

Copyright © Rich Mackin, 2018

The right of Rich Mackin to be identified as
the Author of this work has been asserted in
accordance with the Copyright, Designs and
Patents Act 1988.

ISBN 978 1 4456 7638 8 (print)
ISBN 978 1 4456 7639 5 (ebook)

British Library Cataloguing in Publication Data.
A catalogue record for this book is available from
the British Library.

Origination by Amberley Publishing.
Printed in the UK.

Foreword

Ordered in 1985 as part of the East Coast Main Line electrification, the thirty-one-strong Class 91 fleet was delivered between 1988 and 1991 at BREL's Crewe Works, under subcontract from GEC, Brush and ASEA. After electrification was completed in July 1991, the Class 91s became the backbone of British Rail's fleet, operating between London and Edinburgh, and were originally dubbed 'InterCity 225' due to their intended ability to run at 225 kph (140 mph). In the end they have only operated in service at 125 mph, but to this day they form the principle traction for Virgin Trains East Coast, plying their trade daily on the route they were built to serve, accompanied by Mark 4 coaches built by Metro Cammell.

Today, the Class 91s and Mark 4s face a less certain future. 2018 will see the first Hitachi-built Class 801s enter service, and at the time of writing Virgin intend to keep just seven shortened Mark 4 sets in use for fast services between London and Edinburgh.

This book turns the spotlight on these powerful workhorses and their coaches, documenting all thirty-one members of the Class 91 fleet, as well as the Mark 4 coach fleet, which ply their trade on the East Coast route.

With a covering of snow on the front, East Coast's No. 91101 arrives at Peterborough on 24 March 2013. The Class 91 was painted into a promotional livery when East Coast launched an Up Flying Scotsman service between Edinburgh and London. The purple livery fades into silver at the locomotive's 'No. 2' end.

The rear of Flying Scotsman-liveried No. 91101 is captured in detail, showing how the purple fades to silver to match the coaching stock.

The thistle emblem on No. 91101 is based on the headboard carried by Deltics working the Flying Scotsman service back in BR days. It seen here as the locomotive propels a service out of Darlington on 20 December 2014.

In the final weeks before the franchise is 're-privatised', East Coast's No. 91101 arrives at Darlington on 20 February 2015.

East Coast's No. 91101 *City of York* leaves Darlington on 31 May 2013 with a service to London.

National Express East Coast's No. 91102 speeds through Peterborough on 3 October 2009.

GNER's No. 91103 *County of Lincolnshire* leaves Doncaster with an early evening London service on 16 July 2006.

East Coast's No. 91103 leaves Darlington on 12 July 2010, wearing the 'temporary' livery applied by National Express that became a long-term feature. The vinyl name was removed by National Express, as was the case with all Class 91s, though some had them reapplied in lettering so small it was barely legible.

East Coast's light colours had a tendency to show dirt below the pantograph, caused by wear on the carbon head as it rubs against overhead wires at high speeds. This is evident on No. 91103 as it slows to a stop at Darlington on 21 September 2013.

Virgin's No. 91104 forms a service to Leeds at London King's Cross on 2 September 2017. From the same operator, HST power car No. 43307 can also be seen.

East Coast's No. 91104 sits in Doncaster West Yard on 3 June 2010. The locomotive is awaiting entry to the nearby works for an overhaul.

Damage to the front grille, between the headlights, is visible on No. 91104 as it propels a service out of Darlington on 9 April 2010. The grille is prone to damage from high-speed impacts with birds unfortunate enough to get in the locomotive's way.

GNER's No. 91104 *Grantham* prepares to leave Darlington's Platform 4 with a northbound service on 25 March 2005.

The morning sun shows the vivid red on the side of Virgin's No. 91104 at London King's Cross on 2 September 2017. The Class 91 is leading a departure to Leeds, which was delayed by a coach door not closing properly until staff intervened.

GNER's No. 91105 *County Durham* leaves Darlington on 1 January 2004 during a limited New Year's Day service.

No. 91105 *County Durham* approaches Darlington on 20 April 2004.

GNER's No. 91105 *County Durham* forms a London-bound service at Leeds on 2 September 2005. At this time, Leeds services were covered by HSTs, Class 91s and Class 373 Eurostars.

National Express East Coast's No. 91105 propels a service out of Doncaster on 10 February 2008. The name *County of Durham* has been reapplied on the white stripe, but the lettering is so small it is barely noticeable from a distance.

East Coast siblings Nos 91106 and 91117 *West Riding Limited* call at Newcastle on 26 June 2013. No. 91106 will form a service to London after terminating with a northbound service, while No. 91117 will continue north to Edinburgh.

East Coast's No. 91106 arrives at Darlington on 21 September 2013.

National Express East Coast's No. 91106 forms a southbound service at Newcastle on 16 July 2009.

Four years later, No. 91106 is performing the same duty, this time on 26 June 2013 for a different operator.

GNER's No. 91107 *Newark on Trent* pauses at Darlington with a northbound service on 23 June 2005.

In a light snow flurry, No. 91107 *Newark on Trent* calls at Darlington's Platform 4 on 28 December 2005.

East Coast's No. 91107 caused a stir in 2013 when it was given a special livery to promote the home release of the then latest James Bond film, *Skyfall*. With a matching Mark 4 set, the predominantly white livery provided a striking contrast to the silver, grey and dark blue liveries still in circulation on the Class 91 fleet. It was also temporarily numbered back to 91007 for a short time, and given a cast nameplate. It is seen leading the set on a promotional run at Newcastle on 16 February 2013, the first day it was seen in public.

Later losing the *Skyfall* livery in place of East Coast grey, and then Virgin red and white, No. 91107 speeds through Grantham on 7 April 2017. The locomotive is still named *Skyfall*.

Passing a northbound service just visible on the right, No. 91108 forms the rear of a service at Darlington on 16 May 2014.

Under an overcast sky, No. 91108 propels a London-bound service out of Darlington on 16 May 2014.

Virgin's No. 91108 leads a service past Aycliffe, between Darlington and Durham, on 25 May 2016.

National Express East Coast's No. 91109 calls at wet Doncaster with a northbound service on 13 November 2008.

Virgin's No. 91109 *Sir Bobby Robson* arrives at Darlington on 23 April 2016.

East Coast's No. 91109 *Sir Bobby Robson* forms a service at Newcastle on 16 February 2013. Sir Bobby Robson managed the city's football club between 1999 and 2004, and passed away in 2009.

A closer look at the *Sir Bobby Robson* nameplate fitted to No. 91109. The locomotive was named at Newcastle in March 2011 by his widow Elsie and former Newcastle footballer Alan Shearer.

GNER's No. 91110 *David Livingstone* calls at Darlington with a northbound service on 4 August 2007.

No. 91110 was unveiled in a striking livery commemorating the Battle of Britain Memorial Flight at York's National Railway Museum on 2 June 2012, showing images of the famous Spitfire, Hurricane and Lancaster aircraft and an RAF crest.

Virgin's No. 91110 *Battle of Britain Memorial Flight* is ready to power a service to London on 1 May 2015.

The graphics depicted in No. 91110 *Battle of Britain Memorial Flight*'s striking livery are shown to good effect at Newcastle on 1 May 2015. Also visible on the nearest cab is a small plaque marking the occasion the locomotive reached 162 mph on 17 September 1989.

A closer look at No. 91110's plaque, marking the occasion it reached 162 mph – the fastest speed achieved by a British locomotive.

National Express East Coast's No. 91111 became the sole example of the Class 91 fleet to wear the company's silver/white livery during the two years they held the franchise. It is seen here at Heaton Traction & Rolling Stock Maintenance Depot on 14 September 2008. No Mark 4 coaches were painted in this livery.

Surrounded by extensive renovation work, National Express East Coast's No. 91111 has recently arrived at London King's Cross with a service from the north on the afternoon of 25 May 2009.

No. 91111's National Express livery would later give way to East Coast grey, as seen arriving at Darlington on 17 July 2014.

No. 91111 would wear a second unique livery when it was covered in a vinyl wrap to commemorate 100 years since the start of the First World War, and the lives lost in that conflict. Unveiled in October 2014 and named *For the Fallen*, the nameplate carries the crests of regiments along the East Coast Main Line, while the intricate livery depicts soldiers and tributes commemorating their efforts in the war. It is seen here leaving Darlington on 6 December 2014.

By 2016, No. 91111 carried a revised version of the livery, with the 'East Coast' branding replaced with a small Virgin logo on the No. 2 cab. It is caught on camera at Newcastle on 29 February 2016.

East Coast's No. 91112 leaves Darlington in fading light on a wintry 26 November 2010.

No. 91112 catches the hazy afternoon sun at Darlington on 31 May 2010 as it propels a London-bound service out of the town.

Five months into National Express East Coast's short-lived franchise, No. 91112 *County of Cambridgeshire* leaves Darlington on 7 May 2008 with a London service.

East Coast's No. 91112 has been repainted into the company's grey colour scheme at York's Platform 9 on 21 September 2014, hauling the Sky One promotional rake of coaches.

No. 91113 crosses Darlington South Junction on 21 September 2014 with a southbound service.

GNER's No. 91113 *County of North Yorkshire* arrives at Peterborough on 13 July 2006. The station has since been remodelled with several extra platforms to increase capacity.

With a diagonal red band and Virgin logo covering the East Coast livery, No. 91113 shows the signs of a recent franchise change near Aycliffe on 18 April 2015, and is seen just weeks after Virgin Trains East Coast began operations.

East Coast's No. 91113 leads a northbound service out of York on 14 June 2012.

GNER's No. 91114 *St Mungo Cathedral* leaves Darlington on the rear of a southbound service on 22 May 2004.

With a subtle alteration to East Coast's grey livery, No. 91114 *Durham Cathedral* slows on the approach to Darlington on 16 May 2014.

Despite being partially covered by temporary Virgin branding, No. 91114 *Durham Cathedral*'s livery variation is clearly visible in this view at Newcastle on 2 March 2015. Arches below the purple stripe represent Durham's distinctive viaduct with the silhouette of a Class 91 and Mark 4 set crossing the structure.

With No. 91114 taking the lead, a Mark 4 emerges from the shadows at Newcastle on 29 February 2012 for a crew change before continuing to Edinburgh.

National Express East Coast's No. 91114 leads a northbound working out of York on 22 August 2008. Unusually, the full number has been applied to the cab front below the grille, rather than the usual last two digits.

GNER's No. 91115 *Holyrood* heads north on the centre road at Durham on 31 May 2004. This line is typically used by northbound services that aren't stopping at the station, having just crossed the viaduct depicted on sister locomotive No. 91114.

No. 91115 *Holyrood* powers a London-bound service out of Doncaster on 3 July 2005.

Five months after National Express withdrew from the InterCity East Coast franchise, evidence of both it and previous operator GNER are seen on No. 91115, photographed on 24 April 2010. A white stripe has covered both GNER's red stripe and the names applied to all Class 91 locomotives. The Mark 4 coach behind also has the white stripe, but in common with the rest of the fleet retains the red doors applied by GNER between 2003 and 2005.

East Coast's No. 91115 *Blaydon Races* pushes a London service out of Peterborough on 24 March 2013, during a season of unseasonably cold weather. The locomotive is named after the nineteenth-century folk song popular in and around Newcastle.

A GNER Class 91 leads a northbound service into Doncaster on 9 July 2006. As GNER applied small numbers to the sides of their locomotives, they were often difficult to identify unless the name could be clearly read.

With the recently added white stripe and larger number evident, National Express East Coast's No. 91116 leaves Darlington on 6 May 2008.

A 'not to be moved' sign adorns East Coast's No. 91116 at Newcastle on 28 February 2014. The locomotive is part of a set being cleaned on the platform between services, and will later work to London.

Almost two years to the day later and No. 91116 now wears the vivid colours of Virgin Trains East Coast at Newcastle Central, and will again form a service to London once the coaches have been cleaned and prepared for use.

GNER's No. 91116 *Strathclyde* arrives at Peterborough on 3 July 2006.

As dusk sets in, East Coast's No. 91117 is leading a northbound service at York's Platform 11 on 6 October 2010.

After receiving East Coast grey livery, No. 91117 was one of the first locomotives to be named by the nationalised operator, as *West Riding Limited*, being named after a Bradford–London service introduced by the LNER in 1937. Today, the West Riding Limited is the 06.30 departure from the Yorkshire city.

National Express East Coast's No. 91118 undergoes routine weekend maintenance at Heaton Traction & Rolling Stock Maintenance Depot on 14 September 2008.

Presenting a mismatched appearance with a rake of grey Mark 4 coaches, blue No. 91118 arrives at Darlington on 16 May 2014.

GNER's No. 91118 *Bradford Film Festival* heads a service at Newcastle on 5 November 2006. Unusually, this is a southbound service on Platform 2, which is traditionally used for services heading to Edinburgh and beyond.

On 10 July 2007, No. 91118 *Bradford Film Festival* departs Peterborough with a southbound service.

Under a clear blue sky, East Coast's No. 91119 leaves Darlington on 28 May 2010, with nationalised operator East Coast's logos covering the separate 'National Express' logo and plain 'East Coast' lettering.

On 2 March 2015, the official launch day of Virgin Trains East Coast, No. 91119 was one of a number of Class 91s adorned with a temporary red splash and logo covering the East Coast branding.

With the Sky One Mark 4 rake, No. 91119 speeds through Northallerton on 8 June 2014. The next stop will be Darlington, 14 miles away.

Virgin's No. 91119 propels a London service out of Peterborough on 7 April 2017.

On a wet 2 December 2008, Nos 91120, 91108 and 91114 are lined up at London King's Cross.

National Express East Coast's No. 91120 is ready to lead a service from London to the north at King's Cross on 25 May 2009. From here, Class 91s operate to a variety of destinations, including Leeds, Skipton, York, Newcastle, Edinburgh and Glasgow.

A little over a month into the franchise, and many Virgin Class 91s still carry East Coast grey with temporary Virgin branding, as worn by No. 91120 at York on 5 April 2015. It will be the end of the year before the grey livery is ousted.

With the addition of a white cab roof to reflect heat, Virgin's No. 91121 propels a service out of Darlington on 30 September 2016.

On 8 December 2007, No. 91121 rests at London King's Cross after powering one of GNER's last southbound services. National Express have already applied a white stripe and their own branding to the Class 91.

On the evening of 8 December 2007, No. 91121's duties are finished as it sits at London King's Cross, on the last day of the National Express franchise.

Looking clean despite carrying a very much obsolete livery, No. 91121 is captured at Peterborough on 24 March 2013.

GNER's No. 91122 *Double Trigger* arrives at Edinburgh Waverley on 29 February 2004. St Andrew's House, the headquarters building of the Scottish Government, towers over the station's eastern approach. The locomotive is named after a famous racehorse, continuing the tradition of East Coast Main Line motive power being named in this way.

GNER's No. 91122 is devoid of company branding at London King's Cross on 8 December 2007. The following morning, National Express took over the InterCity East Coast franchise, only to hand it back after less than two years.

Under bright platform lights, East Coast's Nos 91124 and 91119 occupy Platforms 2 and 3 at Newcastle Central on 15 November 2010.

GNER's No. 91124 *Reverend W. Awdry* calls at Darlington on 26 June 2004. The Reverend is best known for writing *The Railway Series*, giving the world Thomas the Tank Engine, among many other classic characters.

No. 91124 *Reverend W. Awdry* propels a non-stop service through Darlington on 28 May 2007.

With the *Reverend W. Awdry* name long removed, Virgin's No. 91124 calls at Peterborough on 7 April 2017.

The late afternoon sun illuminates East Coast's No. 91125 as it leaves Darlington on 20 June 2010. By this point no stock had been repainted in the company's light grey livery, with a Class 91 and rake of Mark 4 coaches adopting the livery a couple of months later.

East Coast re-vinyled No. 91125 and a rake of Mark 4 coaches in a special livery to mark the launch of a television series that went behind the scenes of the operator in 2014. It is seen at Darlington on 16 May 2014.

Where possible, Sky One-liveried No. 91125 was paired up with the matching rake of coaches, and the ensemble is seen leaving Darlington on 16 May 2014.

East Coast's No. 91125 slows to stop at Northallerton on 20 April 2013.

Late in the day, Virgin's No. 91126 leaves Darlington with a service to London on 6 September 2015. A layer of dirt covers the dark grey cab roof. The choice of colours led to the cabs of Class 91s becoming warm, so they were later painted white to reflect heat and aid driver comfort.

With a crudely stencilled number visible on the front of the cab, National Express East Coast's No. 91126 calls at Darlington on 22 November 2008. National Express were halfway through their brief period of operating the franchise at the time, before pulling out the following year.

East Coast's No. 91126 speeds through Northallerton with a service on 20 July 2014. The yellow stripe commonly seen on platforms has been enhanced with further markings as fast trains run through the station at 100 mph. Regular announcements advise the public to stand away from the platform edge as fast trains approach.

Passengers wait to board a train headed by No. 91126 at Peterborough on 24 March 2013, as it slows to a stop at the Cambridgeshire station. With sub-zero temperatures caused by a late cold snap, the passengers were no doubt grateful for the heat and comfort of the Mark 4 coaches!

East Coast pair Nos 91127 and 91125 are captured side-by-side at Newcastle on 26 June 2013.

East Coast's No. 91127 accelerates away from Doncaster with a southbound service on 3 June 2010.

The full length of a Mark 4 rake is visible in this view of East Coast's No. 91127 at Darlington on 2 September 2013. A rake typically consists of a Driving Luggage Van, three first class coaches, a buffet and five standard class coaches.

Virgin's No. 91127 arrives at Newcastle's Platform 4 on 27 March 2017 with a London-bound service.

With ScotRail's No. 158727 for company, GNER's No. 91128 rests at Edinburgh Waverley before forming a service to London on 29 February 2004.

GNER's No. 91128 *Peterborough Cathedral* extends from the shadows at Edinburgh Waverley on 29 February 2004. Class 91s typically operate an hourly service between London and Edinburgh.

Unusually, Virgin's No. 91128 is at the south of a service at Darlington on 28 February 2016, the set running in reverse formation. Just visible on the right is preserved Class 47 No. 47712 in BR ScotRail livery, which, along with No. 47192, had been collected from the Weardale Railway by DCR's No. 31452.

With the distinctive Thorpe Road bridge in the background, Virgin's No. 91128 *INTERCITY 50* arrives at Peterborough on 7 April 2017. The locomotive was named in 2016 to celebrate fifty years since British Rail introduced the iconic 'Inter-City' branding for long-distance trains.

National Express East Coast No. 91129 *Queen Elizabeth II* passes through Doncaster on 13 November 2008. The white stripe eliminated the name once applied to the locomotive, but it was later reapplied in very small blue lettering, barely visible in the above photograph.

East Coast's No. 91129 arrives at Darlington on 20 December 2014 with a northbound service. At this point, the nationalised operator has only a couple of months to go before the franchise returned to the private sector under Virgin Trains East Coast.

East Coast's No. 91130 leaves Doncaster with a working to London on 3 June 2010.

Contrasting with a Mark 4 rake still wearing GNER blue livery, East Coast's recently repainted No. 91130 leaves Darlington on 13 May 2012.

National Express East Coast's No. 91130 leaves the Grade II listed York station on 22 August 2008. The impressive station opened in 1877.

East Coast's No. 91130 pulls into York's Platform 5 on 25 April 2011.

East Coast's GNER blue No. 91131 propels a silver set of Mark 4s out of Darlington on 9 June 2011.

GNER's No. 91131 *County of Northumberland* exchanges passengers at Darlington on 24 September 2006. The previous year, GNER successfully retained the InterCity East Coast franchise, only to hand it back in 2007 due to financial difficulties.

On 23 January 2017, Virgin's No. 91131 calls at Newcastle with a service to Edinburgh.

East Coast's No. 91132 is seen leaving Darlington on 7 May 2012. When the Class 91s went through the 'Delta 91' refurbishment project at Doncaster in the early 2000s, they were renumbered by changing the third digit to a '1'. No. 91132 was the exception to this – built as No. 91023, it was involved in derailments at Hatfield and Great Heck just a few months apart. Harking back to old driver superstitions, it was given an entirely new identity.

East Coast's No. 91132 slows down to stop at Darlington's Platform 4 on 15 February 2013.

In early morning light, East Coast's No. 91132 speeds through Doncaster with a non-stop service.

King's Cross is dominated by GNER Class 91s on 27 December 2003, with no less than four examples lined up at the London terminus. A Class 373 Eurostar set, hired by GNER for services to York and Leeds, can be seen in the background.

DB Cargo's No. 67007 leads a diverted Mark 4 set into Carlisle on 23 September 2017. Engineering work north of Newcastle saw Anglo-Scottish services divert across the Tyne Valley route to the border city, where Class 67s are used to haul a handful of services (the majority are operated by diesel HSTs). The Class 67 will detach here, with No. 91110 propelling the service north to Edinburgh. The locomotive will later haul a London-bound service as far as Newcastle.

East Coast Driving Luggage Van No. 82200 brings up the rear of a service at Doncaster on 28 March 2012. These vehicles were built to carry large items of luggage in the space between the cab and guard's office.

Now repainted into East Coast's grey livery, No. 82200 trails an Edinburgh-bound working out of Newcastle on 26 June 2013.

East Coast DLV No. 82201 leads a London service out of Darlington on 21 May 2011. The light grey dome on the roof is a satellite receiver for the Wi-Fi system fitted to the Mark 4 fleet between 2003 and 2005.

Virgin's vivid red and white livery catches the low autumn sun as No. 82203 leaves Darlington on 6 September 2015.

A week after Virgin Trains took over the InterCity East Coast franchise, most of their fleet showed no sign of the new operator. As the sun drops toward the horizon, No. 82203 leads a service past Northallerton on 7 March 2015.

The driver of East Coast DLV No. 82204 remotely drives a Class 91 on the rear as the set leaves Darlington with a service to London on 31 May 2014.

East Coast painted No. 82205 in a special livery to mark the launch of an Up Flying Scotsman service from Edinburgh to London. Matching locomotive No. 91101, the DLV leads a southbound service out of Darlington on 4 April 2013. The emblem on the end resembles the stylised thistle headboard carried by Flying Scotsman locomotives (usually Deltics) in British Rail days.

Virgin applied their own Flying Scotsman livery to No. 82205, with a subtle Saltire flag applied near the cab end. The DLV is on the rear of a northbound service at Darlington on 29 December 2016.

Freshly repainted No. 82206 leads a London-bound service out of Darlington on 30 September 2011. 125 mph running will soon see a layer of dirt added to the pristine grey, purple and yellow!

On 1 November 2015, Virgin's No. 82207 leads a Mark 4 set out of Darlington.

East Coast's silver-liveried No. 82207 leads a service toward Northallerton on 8 June 2014, on the mostly flat stretch of the East Coast Main Line between Darlington and York.

Virgin's No. 82208 leads a southbound service into Peterborough. For many Virgin services, this is the last stop before London.

Passengers board a southbound service at Darlington, led by DLV No. 82209, on 8 December 2013. West Coast Railway Company Class 47 No. 47746 rests alongside with the empty coaching stock from a charter train. It will later return to the company's Carnforth Depot.

East Coast's No. 82209 was the first to be painted in the company's original silver livery. Still pristine after several months, the DLV brings up the rear of a working at Darlington on 8 January 2011.

East Coast's No. 82210 leads a set into Doncaster's long Platform 3 on 3 June 2010.

With a covering of snow on the ground, East Coast's No. 82211 leads a London-bound service out of Darlington on 5 February 2012.

Virgin's No. 82212 has HST power car No. 43208 *Lincolnshire Echo* for company under the restored roof at London King's Cross on 2 September 2017. The London terminus has seen a transformation in recent years, with the station's façade restored and a spacious new ticket hall built.

East Coast DLV No. 82213 brings up the rear of a northbound working at Doncaster on 28 March 2012.

Sunlight shining through the roof at Darlington casts a pattern of shadows over DLV No. 82213 on 14 June 2009.

The cab roof of DLV No. 82214 demonstrates how light colours make certain liveries harder to keep clean than others as it leaves Darlington on 16 May 2014.

Virgin's No. 82215 shows the temporary branding applied across much of their fleet in the franchise's first months when captured at Darlington on 8 April 2015.

Carrying a distinctive livery to promote a Sky One series that went behind the scenes at East Coast, No. 82216 leads a London-bound service out of Darlington on 16 May 2014.

On the last day of the GNER franchise, No. 82216 is already carrying National Express East Coast branding when seen at London King's Cross on 8 December 2007. The rebranding process was unusual in that it was in full swing several weeks before GNER lost the franchise.

In low winter sun, DLV No. 82217 leads a service into Darlington on 29 December 2013.

In sub-zero temperatures after a late cold snap, No. 82218 forms the rear of a northbound service at Peterborough on 24 March 2013.

National Express East Coast's No. 82219 leads a southbound service out of Darlington on a clear summer day, 14 June 2009.

With East Coast branding covering 'National Express', which was in turn applied over GNER livery, No. 82220 is captured at Darlington on 30 September 2011.

Six months later, in pristine condition, East Coast's No. 82220 accelerates away from Darlington on 27 March 2012.

In comparison, the front of DLV No. 82220 is showing extensive wear and tear at Darlington on 26 October 2015. Virgin's red and white livery had only been applied a few months earlier.

With the city's castle keep as a backdrop, No. 82222 emerges from the curve east of Newcastle Central station as it approaches with a southbound service on 28 February 2014.

With the dark blue of past operator GNER still wearing well, East Coast's No. 82223 heads a southbound service at Darlington on 13 March 2010.

Already showing dirt and wear, Virgin's No. 82223 leaves Darlington on 15 May 2016.

Passionate people.
Passionate places.

north east
england

www.northeastengland.co.uk

82224

GNER applied 'One NorthEast' branding to No. 82224, promoting the now-defunct Regional Development Agency, which existed between 1999 and 2012.

Virgin's No. 82224 arrives at Newcastle's Platform 4 on 27 March 2017.

East Coast's grey livery had a tendency to show dirt around the buffer beam, evident from the brown marks on No. 82225 as it departs Darlington on 19 July 2013.

On 23 January 2017, No. 82225 trails an Edinburgh service out of Newcastle.

More than two years after the nationalised operator East Coast took on the InterCity East Coast franchise, GNER's dark blue livery was still evident, despite it becoming obsolete when National Express took over the franchise in 2007. Here, DLV No. 82226 is captured at Darlington on 25 March 2012.

The dark blue of former operator GNER is still presentable, even with the red stripe replaced by white, as No. 82227 slows to stop at Doncaster on 25 March 2012.

Virgin's No. 82206 passes Class 800 No. 800101 at Darlington on 24 February 2017. The nine-car 'Azuma' set is on a test run, with the Hitachi-built trains due to enter service at the end of 2018.

On a bright spring day, No. 82229 leads a non-stop East Coast service through Northallerton on 20 April 2013.

The '007' branding can still be seen on No. 82231 at Newcastle nearly a year later, on 2 March 2015. This was one of the first DLVs to carry Virgin branding on top of the now-obsolete East Coast livery. Virgin had taken over the franchise the previous day, and this was the official launch, it being the first weekday into the new franchise.

An image of Daniel Craig as James Bond adorns the side East Coast's No. 82231 at Newcastle on 16 February 2013, the DLV being part of a set used to promote the DVD/Blu-ray release of the movie *Skyfall*.

An unidentified GNER DVT leads a set out of Darlington on a London-bound service on 27 June 2005.

The interior of a freshly refurbished Mark 4 Standard Open (End), showing the partition that separated the smoking area. This was abolished around this time as the operators that still permitted smoking gradually phased it out.

The new seats fitted to a Mark 4 Standard Open during the 2003–05 'Mallard' refurbishment.

National Express branding was applied to the GNER Mark 3 and Mark 4 coaches prior to that franchise ending. On 8 December 2007, a Mark 4 Standard Open (End) was partially re-liveried while between services at King's Cross. This led to many sets only being re-branded on one side as the staff applying the vinyls were working on the platform. The end vehicle is lacking a corridor connection at one end, and couples directly to a Class 91 locomotive.

Still painted in GNER base blue, National Express East Coast Mark 4 buffet car No. 10309 provides the catering on a London-bound service at Darlington on 7 May 2008. These coaches were built with first class accommodation for an onboard restaurant service until 2003–05, when refurbished examples were turned out with standard class seating, a First Open being used as dedicated restaurant seating.

Skyfall-liveried Mark 4 buffet No. 10317's kitchen-side body provides a background for the large '007' logo to appear mostly uninterrupted at Newcastle on 16 February 2013, on the redecorated set's debut run.

National Express East Coast Mark 4 First Open No. 11241 leaves Peterborough on a northbound service on 3 October 2009. These vehicles were dedicated restaurant coaches from 2003 to 2005, until dining services were discontinued.

East Coast Mark 4 First Open No. 11292 shows off the nationalised operator's austere grey livery at Peterborough on 24 March 2013.

Low sun illuminates East Coast First Open No. 11320 at Darlington, 19 April 2014.

First Open No. 11322 leaves Darlington with a service to London on 23 September 2013.

With the National Express branding replaced by East Coast's, First Open No. 11412 is the leading passenger vehicle on a London-bound service at York, 3 July 2011.

Skyfall-liveried Standard Open (End) No. 12204 forms a service at Newcastle on 16 February 2013, the first outing for the promotional livery. These vehicles differ from normal Standard Opens by lacking a corridor connection on the end, and being fitted with a drophead buckeye coupler. They also feature an internal partition which used to separate a smoking area from the rest of the coach. GNER banned smoking on all services midway through the 'Mallard' refurbishments, rendering the partitions redundant.

National Express East Coast's No. 12205 forms part of a service terminating at Newcastle on 9 August 2008.

Sky One advertising coach No. 12217 was part of a set re-vinyled to promote a television series that went behind the scenes at East Coast. Each coach showed a different frontline staff member at the operator.

GNER's Standard Open End No. 12231 has been de-branded at London King's Cross on 8 December 2007. With all branding removed, new decals for the number have been applied, replacing the small blue numbers (displayed on the red stripe) with larger, clearer white numbers. The Class 91 at the far left of the photograph has had the white stripe applied over the red.

East Coast Standard Open (Disabled) No. 12310 approaches York on 5 April 2015. When built, these were the first British Rail coaches to feature accessible toilets and wheelchair spaces, and are marshalled next to the buffet coach.

Standard Open (Disabled) No. 12322 advertises Sky One's East Coast series at Darlington on 16 May 2014.

East Coast's original livery, applied to a handful of Mark 4 sets in 2010, featured a purple stripe against a silver background. This proved difficult to keep clean, with repainted stock looking shabby after a short time in service. No. 12327 was one of the few painted in this livery, still wearing it at Darlington on 28 February 2015.

Light grey-painted Standard Open No. 12405 leaves Darlington with a southbound service on 31 May 2014.

The bright interior of a refurbished Mark 4 shows the new seat covers, carpets and interior signage applied by Virgin shortly after they took over the franchise. This new look is set to be short-lived when Hitachi-built Class 801s replace them in 2018/19.

None of National Express East Coast's Mark 4 coaches wore the company's silver and white livery, instead retaining GNER dark blue with a white stripe applied. Standard Open No. 12415 shows this livery at Darlington on 15 July 2008.

Skyfall-liveried Standard Open No. 12457 arrives at Newcastle on 16 February 2013.

East Coast's No. 12464 was part of the set that wore a Sky One promotional livery during the first half of 2014. It was captured at Darlington on 16 May of that year.

Wearing a combination of three liveries (GNER, National Express and East Coast), Standard Open No. 12466 is part of a northbound service at York on 31 March 2013.

Still wearing the base blue of GNER, Standard Open No. 12476 calls at Doncaster on 3 June 2010.